# How to Care for Your Degu

## Contents

*Photographs by Martin Eustace, Diane Griffiths-Irwin, Paul Davis, Carolyn Gill, Mike Jordan and Frank Naylor*

*Degus for Martin Eustace's photos kindly provided by Melanie Sitch*

KINGDOM

# INTRODUCTION

The degu, latin name *Octodon degu*, is a member of the family Octodontidae. The latin name is derived from the worn enamel surface of its teeth which forms a pattern in the shape of a figure eight.

Degus originate from Chile, living in habitats ranging from coastal scrublands to rocky outcrops at around 3,000 metres elevation. The degu is resistant to the severe cold and high winds of the mountains; they dislike extreme heat, and wet and damp conditions. Living in groups of up to 100 members, degus are exceptionally good diggers. They build complex burrows up to one metre deep, containing nests and food stores. The burrows usually have several entrances and exits. In their homeland they are regarded as a pest because they destroy crops and plantations. In ideal conditions degus will breed prolifically, eating all that is in their path. Like squirrels, degus hoard food supplies. Wild degus may have a lifespan of only one or two years because they are the prey of many different animals, such as birds and snakes. In captivity, they are more likely to reach 7-10 years. Females frequently die at an earlier age than their male counterparts; perhaps this is because breeding large litters can be a drain on them. Having said that, I (DGI) met a lady on a flight from Amsterdam to Heathrow who claimed to have a degu aged fourteen and a half! She said that her family (Mother, Father, herself and two brothers) were given three degus by their next door neighbour, a zoo employee, who was moving to

**A degu in the wild at the entrance to his burrow.**

a flat and could no longer keep them. The 3 degus were soon joined by 2 more because the parents liked their children's new pets so much!

Degus were first discovered in the eighteenth century and were originally thought to be members of the squirrel family. More recently, they have also been likened to gerbils and chinchillas. Originally, a small number of degus were exported from their native homeland to be used for medical research into diabetes, a disease to which they are very prone. Over the years degus have found their way into the pet trade and are becoming very popular. One reason for this may be that they are active during the day and sleep at night, unlike other rodents such as hamsters and mice, which are nocturnal.

A degu will grow to around the same size as a rat, with a head and body length of up to 10-12 inches long and adult weight of around 300 grammes. They have a long tail which ends in a tuft. Degus raise their tail slightly when walking. The tail is very easily detached and extreme care should be exercised at all times. NEVER pick up a degu by the tail.

The degu coat is very dense and mid to dark brown in colour. The stomach area is cream coloured and they also have cream circles around the eyes. Ears are medium to large in size and are rounded. The hindlegs are short with five digits on each whilst the forelegs are longer and have four digits. Degus have long whiskers and yellow/orange teeth. This discolouring is due to a reaction that takes place between the chlorophyll contained in green food and an enzyme in their bodies. The result is an orange organic fluid in their saliva.

## Housing

The degu that you have just purchased from your pet shop or breeder will probably be little more than a freshly weaned infant. You should bear this in

**Degus should be housed in the largest enclosure you can afford.**

mind when purchasing your new pet's permanent accommodation. This small animal will soon grow to be the size of a domestic rat and will be extremely active. If possible, buy or build the largest cage you can afford because degus are very good climbers and this will assist in their need to keep fit and active. A cage with several layers will allow your animal to explore and spend his day in different parts of his territory. The cage should ideally be sited where the degu will feel involved in the hustle and bustle of the owner's life. Degus are also very sociable creatures (as discussed elsewhere in this book) and should therefore be kept in pairs or larger numbers. A single degu may be more prone to disease and may become depressed on his own.

To introduce a new degu to an existing one, divide the cage into two, putting one degu in each section. After a week the degus will be used to the smell of each other and can be allowed to mix. They may fight for a short while to establish who is boss but should settle down after this. If not, they will have to be separated and housed in different cages. Note that two male degus are more likely to get on if they are litter brothers who have been kept together since birth. To increase the chances of two males getting along it is best not to have females within smelling distance, which might cause the males to fight.

Never buy any cage for your degu that has a plastic base area. Degus are notorious chewers and will soon eat their way out of this type of cage, leaving the owner with the expense of buying yet another home for their pet. For the same reason, avoid placing anything made of plastic in your degu's cage, such as ladders, toys or nest boxes, as they will chew it to bits!

There are two types of caging that we would recommend for housing your degu. The first is the all-mesh chinchilla cage and the second is the all-glass aquarium. It is very easy to add branches and toys to the chinchilla cage. The size of cage I (JD) personally use to house an adult pair of degus measures 36 inches (900mm) high, 20 inches (500mm) wide and 18 inches (450mm) deep. I must add though, as a cautionary note, that if you use this type of cage the mesh shelves must be covered with wood. Alternatively, metal sheet floors are also safe for your degu to walk on and will be resistant to chewing, unlike wood. The main aim is to prevent your animal from getting foot sores or a disease known as 'bumblefoot', both of which are caused by the animal constantly walking on mesh. If you wish to keep anything permanently in the cage, think 'metal', for example metal ladders are great for travelling from one floor to the next.

Always ensure that whatever type of enclosure you use for your pet degu, it has very secure fitting doors. Degus are natural escape artists and can prove to be extremely difficult to catch once on the loose!

If you decide to house your degu in an aquarium, the minimum size that I (JD) recommend is 36 inches (900mm) long, 12 inches (300mm) wide and 15 inches (375mm) high. I have found with my own degus that it is advisable to fit a mesh extension to any aquarium that you use. This is dual purpose - it literally

Two examples of all-mesh cages.
The cage pictured above has several floors, allowing the degu plenty of room to explore.
The large cage on the left contains branches which the degu can use for gnawing and climbing.

doubles the area your degu has to run around in and also makes it so much easier to attach branches and toys.

If you wish to add branches to the enclosure, only use those from fruit trees such as apple, pear and so on. The degus will use them to gain access to other levels in their cage and will have great fun clambering up and down, whilst exercising their feet and limbs in the process. Leave the bark on the branches as degus will have hours of fun removing it all and stripping it back to the bare wood. Always check that the branches are clean and free from parasites such as red spider mite. This can be done by leaving the branches to soak in hot water. It is essential for a degu to have something to chew on, so branches and/or a pumice stone will be invaluable in wearing their teeth down. Overgrown teeth can be disastrous for a degu. Degus also love to carry twigs around, sometimes the twig being as large as the degu itself!

Another useful addition is a platform shelf, sited at the top of the cage, which the degus can use for sleeping or sunbathing on. The cardboard inner tubes from toilet and kitchen rolls are also popular - degus love to run through or chew them. A large rough stone placed in a prominent part of the cage can be used by the animals to wear their nails down, which is much easier than the owner trying to clip them.

Most degu owners are unsure whether or not to put a wheel in the enclosure. If you do decide to use a wheel, ensure that it is the *closed* type rather than the open tread type. With the open type of wheel it is very easy for the degu's tail to get caught and be ripped off. As previously stated, the tails do not re-grow. There is some debate about whether the loss of the tail affects the degu's balance and other abilities. I (JD) have found that it is not detrimental to the degu because he soon learns to adapt to having a shorter tail. The stumpy tail is then used for balancing and communicating.

It is also a good idea to provide a wooden nestbox which can be used as a retreat, a sleeping area and something to clamber on. If you fill it with hay and paper tissue for additional bedding, the degus will be in heaven!

Like chinchillas, degus enjoy rolling

Degus are very active creatures and will appreciate a variety of safe toys and items to play with.

and playing in a dust bath. Either chinchilla dust or sand will suffice and giving them this for half an hour once or twice a week will help to keep their skin and fur healthy and in good condition.

## Substrate and Bedding

Degus will need to be cleaned out at least once a week. They need to be cleaned out regularly because they drink large amounts of water which is then converted into urine. However, degus do not smell as much as mice or rabbits.

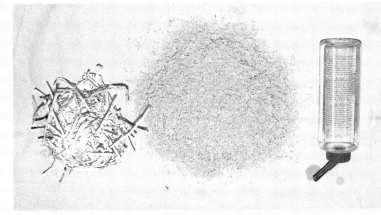

Left to right: Shredded paper, wood shavings and a water bottle.

Whether you house your degu in a cage or aquarium, I (JD) have found that using good quality dust-extracted woodshaving gives the best results. I strongly advise against the use of sawdust because degus are prone to respiratory system irritation which, in turn, leads to breathing difficulties caused by the very fine dust particles found in sawdust. These particles have been known to be fatal to rodents, especially youngsters.

I would also advise against the use of peat as a substrate in your pet's enclosure. The closed environment of a cage or aquarium means that waste liquid such as the animal's urine cannot freely drain away, so the peat eventually becomes water-logged. Once this has happened, sores and infections quickly set in and can be difficult to treat.

Degu urine is very strong and pungent so any build-up in the housing will soon give off an offensive aroma. This is another reason for using woodshavings - they are absorbent and can be changed very quickly and easily.

You may find it helpful to clean your aquarium in the following manner:
• Remove the animal(s), branches, toys etc so that you are left with just an aquarium full of woodshavings.

- Use a dust pan to remove the majority of the soiled woodshavings.
- Remove the last traces of the woodshavings using a vacuum cleaner.
- Wash the aquarium thoroughly, using a general purpose disinfectant.
- Dry and leave to air for a short length of time.
- Whilst the aquarium is airing, wash down all the contents such as food dishes, water bottles, soiled branches and so on.
- When everything is thoroughly dry, add a good deep layer of clean woodshavings and then replace the contents.
- Finally, return the degus to their home.

One problem you may encounter when using aquariums is staining on the glass caused by the degu's strong urine. I have tried many ways to remove this staining and I have found the only successful method is to use a mild de-scaling liquid of the type used for cleaning sink tops. When the aquarium is empty, I apply the de-scaler directly to the staining and leave it to work for at least 15

A pumice stone or rock will help to keep teeth and nails down to a suitable length
(see also page 33).

minutes. This is usually long enough to remove all but the most stubborn of stains, which require a second application. I then thoroughly wash the aquarium with hot water and a washing-up liquid to ensure all traces of de-scaler have been removed.

In the wild, degus line their nests by foraging for dried grass and leaves. Obviously you cannot simulate this very easily in your pet's enclosure. However, I have found that all of the following can give good results:

**Straw**
Straw is a very good substitute for the dried grasses your degu would use in his natural habitat. It is cheaply and easily obtained from pet shops. I have found from past experience that it is false economy to buy straw directly from farm yards. On a farm, straw is usually stored in open barns and is extremely

susceptible to parasitic invasion, both from insects and wild animals. The straw can also be infected by the faeces and urine of wild rodents such as mice, voles and rats.

## Hay

Good quality hay is vital. It is used by the animal for bedding and is an essential part of his diet.

Once again, extreme care must be exercised when choosing a source for your hay supply. Farm-bought hay tends to contain not only hay but an assortment of thistles and wild plants.

The pre-packed hay that you purchase from reputable pet shops has usually been graded, cleaned and prepared for use by pets. Buying hay this way may cost a little more but it is worth the extra few pence involved to keep your degu happy and healthy.

## Shredded paper

You can either purchase shredded paper from pet shops or make your own from magazines and newspapers. Another choice of paper bedding is soft tissue. This can be purchased from your pet shop or you can make your own by shredding paper tissues.

## Fluffy bedding

When a degu gives birth it can be very difficult to decide which type of bedding is the most suitable to use. I have tried all the types of bedding listed above and the only one that I would strongly advise against using is the fluffy cotton wool type of bedding. This is because when baby degus are born they are covered in blood and mucus and fluffy bedding readily sticks to the babies, becoming extremely difficult to remove. The easiest way to remove it is to use plain lukewarm water and soft cotton wool. Dip the cotton wool in warm water, squeeze out the excess and very gently wipe the baby's skin. Repeat until all of the bedding is removed. Please remember, though, that the baby's skin is very fragile and the mother will be very protective so you must carry out this procedure as quickly as possible. I recommend using the soft tissue bedding for babies.

## Handling

Although a degu is roughly the same size as a domestic rat, they must be handled far more delicately. This does not mean that you have to handle your degu wearing kid gloves but some care must be exercised. The majority of degus do not like being over-handled, although there is always the exception to any rule.

If you get a newly weaned infant degu and handle him on a daily basis you may be lucky and get him hand tame. By that I mean that the degu will come onto your hand and not attempt to escape.

I have found that no two degus are ever the same, each has their own individual characteristics and ways. Degus are intelligent and they soon learn to recognise their owner.

I (DGI) have found my degus to be completely fascinated by, and trustworthy with, children. I think this is because degus are so nosey, they love to be at the centre of things. Of course, always supervise children with any type of pet. We have a drawbridge cage door which allows the animals to come out of the cage to be stroked and fed titbits. Degus very seldom bite unless they are terrified, which can be caused by poor handling. (Tetanus jabs should, however, be kept up to date as a precaution.) Never attempt to grab your degu from above (which would be similar to how a predator would act in the wild) or chase him if he escapes. Stay calm and move slowly when handling your pets, and talk to them for reassurance. Degus enjoy being petted and having their ears and noses scratched. Mine also like to be rubbed under their armpit with one or two fingers. However, most do not like being handled all the time, so be respectful of this. If not, overhandling could cause your pet to run and hide when you approach the cage.

When given regular attention, degus seem to bond very quickly with their

Some typical play items: an enclosed wheel, tubing, a wood block, ragger rope and ball. Beware, plastic items will probably be chewed!

**Degus usually bond very quickly with their owners.**

owners. They are extremely inquisitive, energetic and entertaining. In short, they are wonderful to watch! A friendly degu will take his favourite treat from your hand, or jump straight into his food bowl, as mine do. They also have a very good memory, remembering anyone who has teased them or treated them well. If you feed them something outside of the normal feeding time, they will often wait to be given the treat at the new time again the next day.

When handling your degu, always use both hands. Your left hand should be placed underneath the degu to fully support his body whilst your right hand should be used to lightly restrain the animal. By using this method your degu will feel secure and the risk of your degu jumping out of your hands and hurting himself will be greatly reduced. Never ever make a quick grab from above because you may trigger the degu's defence mechanism.

It is worth stating again - **never** pick up or grab a degu by the tail. Degus have a built-in escape mechanism so that, in the wild, should a predator attack, the degu has a chance to get away by shedding the tail skin. This usually leaves the predator sufficiently confused for long enough to allow the degu to make good his escape.

If you do make the mistake of grabbing your degu's tail and you find yourself left holding just the outer sheath of what once was the tail, take your degu to the vet straight away. The degu will be left with just exposed bones; these need to be removed under surgery and the wound stitched. When part of a tail is shed, there is always a lot of bleeding. This could easily cause the degu to bleed to death if he does not receive urgent attention.

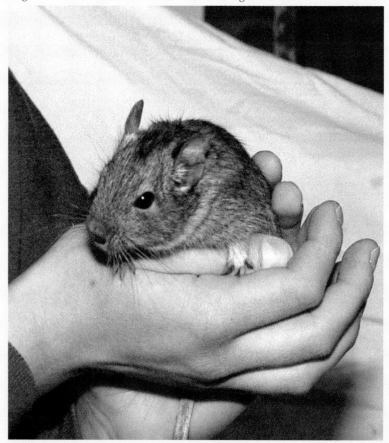

Always use both hands when holding your degu.

These Devon schoolchildren were delighted to be given a pair of degus by Diane Griffiths-Irwin.

# FEEDING

Once a tail is lost it never ever grows back. The degu is left with a stump instead of a nice long tufty tail although, as stated earlier, this does not seem detrimental to the animal.

Finally, on the subject of handling, you may find that your degu 'greets' your fingers gently with his teeth. He is not biting you but it may come as a surprise the first time it happens!

## Feeding

There is a lot of controversy when it comes to feeding degus, with most owners being very confused as to what exactly a degu should or should not be fed.

Unlike most other pets, there are no ready made mixes specifically for degus available for purchase at the time of writing. So it is up to the individual owner to buy the right types of food and mix them himself (see below). Do read the labels on the bags of food you intend to buy for your degu. You will be amazed how many foods are rich in sugar and fats and, although a very small amount of sugar will cause no long term damage to your degu, a lot of sugar certainly will. Degus are extremely susceptible to becoming diabetic because their bodies cannot naturally dispose of sugar. Degus were originally exported from their native homelands to be used in research work on diabetes because they are so prone to this disease.

**Suitable food items for degus.**

(Above) food can be used to assist with taming, and
(below) food dishes should be made of a suitable material.

Never give degus any kind of fruit because most fruits are rich in sugar. I have known many people feed their degus on raisins, apples, pears and so on but, as discussed above, the animal cannot naturally deal with this sugar and the inevitable happens with the degu becoming diabetic. Humans can cope with this condition by giving themselves daily insulin injections but the average pet owner would find it an impossible task to give their degu the insulin injections that it needed. This unfortunately means that any degu that becomes diabetic usually dies within a short space of time.

Another important point to bear in mind when keeping degus is the quality of water supplied. Degus should *not* be given tap water because most domestic water supplies are high in chlorine which is something else that the degu's body cannot deal with naturally. In the wild, their natural diet consists of roots, tubers and grasses whilst drinking water is obtained from rock pools and puddles.

I (JD) use bottled still spring water for my degus and I always read the label on the bottle to ensure that the chlorine level is as low as possible. Bottled water is cheap to buy and is easy to store in a refrigerator. One article I have read recommends that you use tap water and de-chlorinate it by using a low percentage of bleach. To me this practice would be totally unacceptable as it would be easy to get the concentration levels wrong whilst plastic water bottles would absorb the bleach, leading to a build up of levels over a period of time. Bottled water is a cheap and acceptable alternative.

I keep my degus on a strict diet which I know to be both safe and nutritious for them. As a staple diet I feed a mixture of chinchilla pellets and guinea pig

**Bottled spring water contains the least amount of chlorine.**

pellets and I supplement this mixture with Supreme Reggie Rat food (which is low in sugar and fat ), dried carrot, small amounts of bread sticks, small amounts of crusty bread and alfalfa cubes. As a real treat (say, once a week) I occasionally allow my degus an unsalted peanut or a sunflower seed.

Ceramic food dishes are the best to use as you will find that any kind of plastic dish will be quickly demolished by your degu.

My degus (DGI) hoard their food supplies in their wood piles and bedding. They will also take pieces of carrot out of my hand if they feel I am not feeding them quickly enough. Their diet includes rabbit food, guinea pig food, alfalfa, soya, peas, field beans, oats, locust beans, wheat, beat pulp and dried or fresh carrot. Fifty per cent of the diet comes from chinchilla pellets. At present, there is no pet food company that manufactures degu food, so it is up to the owner to provide the appropriate diet. Avoid giving fruit, biscuits and cake because all contain sugar which the degu cannot digest. I also avoid food which is high in carbohydrate (such as corn, cereals and so on). Peanuts, walnuts, hazelnuts, and brazil nuts are all fattening, as are sunflower and pumpkin seeds, so feed sparingly if at all. Potato skin and the green parts of potatoes should not be fed to your degu either.

Degus seem to make a career out of begging for treats. It is important not to give in all the time since they are so small that they easily become fat.

## Breeding

Sexing degus is definitely a matter of practice and experience. Female degus are usually larger than males. Males have interabdominal testes so there is no scrotum to help determine the sex of a degu. To the uninitiated both sexes appear the same as both have a small cone shaped appendage hanging down between the back legs. This is not a sexual organ, it is used for urinating only.

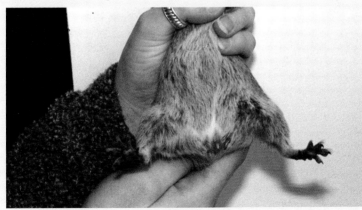

A female degu.

A male degu (see below for details on sexing).

On females the space between the anus and the vagina is very close together but on the male the space between the penis and the anus is further apart (approximately 6 to 10mm). As the female matures, the urethra becomes more inverted whilst in the male it takes on more of a penile shape. Like all things, sexing degus is difficult to start with but does become quite easy with practice.

If you have a male that you do not intend to use for breeding, it is far kinder to have him neutered if he is to be kept with females. It is a much quicker and simpler operation to have the male neutered than to subject the female to a full hysterectomy. The latter is a more complex operation, the animal is under anaesthetic for longer and, as with all small rodents, the risk of death from anaesthetics is higher. The cost of the operation on a female is also usually more expensive too.

With a male, recovery is usually a lot quicker as there may only be two or three dissolvable stitches. It is very important to ensure that the wound is kept thoroughly clean to lessen the risk of infection; you will see your degu constantly cleaning the area. During this period of recovery it is also important to make sure that the degu's enclosure is kept as clean as possible. I completely remove and clean everything in the enclosure twice a week to ensure this is so.

Sometimes, no matter how thorough you are with hygiene, infection still sets in and should this happen the animal should be returned to your veterinary surgeon so that antibiotics can be administered. It is also a good idea to keep the male separate from the other degus that he normally lives with until the scar has totally healed. If the male is returned too soon it is possible that the other degus in the enclosure could pull out the stitches. The male would then have to undergo another operation to have the wound re-stitched. Although degus generally handle anaesthetic very well it is possible that two doses within a short space of time could result in the death of your degu.

After being anaesthetised it is perfectly normal for your degu to stagger around and sway from side to side. His eyes may also appear glazed but all these symptoms should disappear over the next few days. If you have any concerns contact your veterinary surgeon for advice.

Degus are not monogamous and will mate with most other degus of the opposite sex. Very occasionally, they will not like the partner that you have chosen for them but fortunately this is a rare event. If this does happen, separate them and try re-introducing them at a later stage. Should they fight again, they simply do not like each other and should be kept separate. However, if they do get along keep an eye on them for the first week or so. Never put two male degus together with a female or females. There would be a great deal of friction as males compete for any suitable female. The fighting can become very vicious, so my advice is only ever to keep one male with a female or females.

Male degus can become mature and start breeding from the age of ten weeks but some take a lot longer; no two degus are the same. It is more likely that males become sexually mature aged 6-12 months old, depending upon climate and other factors. Females can come into season from 3 months onwards but some may not become sexually mature until nearer 12 months old. Once a female becomes sexually mature the seasons occur around every 30 days. The female's pattern of behaviour does change during the season. She becomes more aggressive and is far less tolerant of the male. There is a lot of tail swishing and a great deal of noise.

A courting couple may warble and lick each other's faces. Eventually, when the female is ready to mate, she will stand for the male, raising her hindquarters to facilitate entry by the male. Copulation only lasts for a few seconds but the act is repeated over and over again, sometimes going on for hours at a time. Male degus certainly have stamina! The male may also sit and brag about it by warbling for hours afterwards

After mating the pair will rest and may then start all over again for several more hours. If the male has a harem he will quite happily service every female as she becomes receptive. Quite often the females will give birth close together and each will have her own nesting space although occasionally one female may allow another female to nest with her.

Degus can breed throughout the year and are sexually mature for around six years. The length of gestation averages 90-93 days but it is often very difficult

**Baby degus are born fully furred and with their eyes open.**

to tell whether a degu is pregnant or not. With a female rat, the belly area extends as the pregnancy advances but this is not common with degus. I (JD) have had females give birth to quite large litters without my knowing that they were pregnant. If a female degu is asleep on her side you may notice the babies moving inside her and this will probably be the only indication that she is pregnant. Sometimes you may notice a swelling in her nipples and there might be a slight loss of blood prior to birth but this once again varies from individual to individual. To avoid the possibility of accidental abortion, it is best to be very gentle with a pregnant female as they appear to be quite fragile during this period.

Once labour starts and the female is having contractions, it should take no longer than 45 minutes for her to deliver all of the babies. At birth the babies will be covered with mucus which the mother normally removes. The litter size can vary between 1 and 10, with 6 being produced on average. I (DGI), in common with other breeders, have found that quite often the first couple of litters from a female will contain only male pups. The mother has four pairs of teats that the pups will scramble to get on. The female will lie over her young to suckle them.

When the pups are born they arrive fully developed, unlike most rodent babies which are born bald, blind and not yet fully formed. Degu babies are fully furred, eyes open and, within a very short space of time, they are usually walking around, even if it is very shakily. Although the eyes are open from birth it usually takes a day or two before the pup can focus properly. The fur is silk-like and the pups are perfect miniatures of the parents. However, no matter how adorable you think the pups are, avoid handling them until they are weaned (around the 4-6 week stage). The mother degu is very protective, and handling of the pups may result in her rejecting or even killing her own litter. Once the mother is relaxed in your presence, handling baby degus is an excellent way of taming them for their new owners, ensuring that they enjoy being handled and are not afraid of humans. It is also useful to be able to demonstrate to potential new owners how to handle degus, both young and adult.

The male degu is usually quite maternal and he plays an important part in rearing the pups. You will often see him keeping the pups warm, grooming them, and rounding them up and returning them to the nest when they stray. He may also play with the pups as they get older, allowing them to climb and jump on him.

I (DGI) have also found that if other females are present in the cage, they seem to act as midwives to the pregnant degu. If there is more than one

**They soon find their feet...**

Top: the average degu litter size is six.
Above: the babies are perfect miniatures of their parents.

mothering degu, they will put their pups in the same nest and share the feeding duties, not appearing to mind which pup belongs to which parent.

The parents will usually mate again soon after the birth and the only way of preventing an endless stream of babies is to either remove the male or have him neutered. It is really up to the pet owner to choose a method but no responsible owner allows their animals to breed continuously as it puts a tremendous strain on the female and inevitably shortens her life.

The pups grow rapidly and by about four weeks old they will be eating solids. They start investigating their environment and every item in their

It is best to avoid disturbing the nest until the babies have been weaned.

enclosure becomes a toy. They will quite happily play with the water bottle and rapidly discover that they can get a drink from it. They also learn a lot of the behaviour that they use throughout their lives by watching and copying their parents.

During the first few weeks following the birth of the pups, the female will only leave the nest area to eat, drink and carry out her toilet functions. As the pups get older the female's time away from the nest lengthens and, by the time the pups are fully weaned, the mother has more or less lost interest.

Do not make the mistake of removing the pups too early. A lot of breeders remove them at around 4 weeks of age but I (JD) personally tend to leave the babies until they are between 5 and 6 weeks old. By this age the pups are fully weaned and tend to fare a lot better when separated finally from their parents. When you remove the babies from their parents, you should separate the sexes to prevent the risk of related animals mating. Inbreeding degus is strongly discouraged by all reputable breeders as it can produce animals with genetic defects and lowered immune systems. Separating the sexes at around six weeks old should prevent poor quality animals being born in the future.

It is your responsibility to ensure that your degus go to good homes only. When prospective buyers call, ask them what they already know about degus and if they are willing to provide the special diet that they require to keep them healthy. Make owners aware that this is an intelligent and active animal which will benefit from human interaction and a stimulating environment. Not much has been published on degus but the Internet is a possible source of information. If you find it difficult to get good homes for the babies, do not breed again from them immediately. It would be better to pair the male off with a son, and a daughter with the mother, so they all have company.

## Behaviour

Degus are really busy little creatures and will give their owners hours of enjoyment. Since degus are very sociable animals, it is kinder to keep at least two degus together. The degu motto seems to be "The more the merrier."

Unlike the majority of rodents, degus are not nocturnal. They sleep during most of the night-time period, usually only leaving the nest to eat, drink or urinate. They tend to catnap throughout the day as well but the sleep periods are broken by long spells of activity. Being active during the day and sleeping at night should fit in well with the routine of most owners.

Although all species of rodent exhibit that they have intelligence to some degree, degus seem to be far more intelligent than any other species. They are very adept at working out how to get out of their enclosure and they have a very good memory. If an event upsets a degu or if you do something that your degu strongly dislikes, the animal will remember it for a very long time.

One of the female degus that I (JD)have at present came to me as a rescue and although I do not know the history of this animal it is obvious that a man has done something to upset her in the past. If a man approaches her cage, she gets extremely defensive and stands upright, squeaking very loudly. When the man moves away from the cage, she settles back down almost immediately.

On the subject of fear response, we (DGI) have a cross feral cat called Tiggy who is completely disinterested in the degus but something about her black and grey striped coat seems to trigger a survival response in them. When they see her, the alarm call goes up from Digger, the male degu, which sends the youngsters scurrying down the 3 tiers to hide in their massive pile of bedding. Meantime, Digger is joined by Salt and Pepper, his two wives, and they all make so much noise that they nearly fall off the nestbox they are sitting on!

Degus in the wild have a very complex social structure. A male degu usually have his own harem of females, which can number up to twenty. A male's social standing is measured by the height of a pile of twigs he collects and builds at the entrance to his burrow. If two male degus become involved in a territory dispute it is quite a vicious affair which ends up in a fight. The loser may be either severely or fatally injured. It is not advisable to house two males together with females in the same cage. It will only be a matter of time before fights break out and the end result could be that you end up with one of the males being killed by the other.

Degus have a very complicated method of communication. This involves the use of both verbal sounds and body movements. The vocal sounds range from a low warbling noise up to a high pitched whistle. When frightened or upset, a degu will emit a high pitched 'wheep' sound which it makes in rapid succession and which can last for several hours.

When a degu is happy or relaxed you will hear a chuckling noise which is sometimes accompanied by whistling. Some of my degus (JD) will whistle back to me when I whistle them and one female I have has almost managed to mimic a wolf whistle successfully.

**Ready to sound the alarm if necessary.**

**Degus do not often quarrel over food, except perhaps when treats are around!**

My (DGI) degus will often sing and chirp to the blackbirds or to each other; they also sing to baby degus which are only a few hours old. I find the chirpy sounds enchanting.

Sometimes the chuckling sound will be slightly more enthusiastic than usual and this often denotes the prelude to mating. Body language is used extensively in degu communication and the new degu keeper will learn in time what each noise and each body movement means.

Two degus living in the same enclosure, especially if they are male and female, tend to get on very well together with very few arguments or disagreements. Treats seem to provoke what is probably the most visual and verbal display by degus. They do not like sharing their treats with each other and you will probably notice a lot of tail shaking, turning away from each other and running to opposite ends of the enclosure. These actions are always accompanied by lots of noise, ranging from low squeaks to full high pitched screams. Although this looks and sounds extremely aggressive, I (JD) have never witnessed any injuries during this performance. The dominant degu may also monopolise the food bowl by sitting in it and refusing to let the others near. A degu will rarely bite a person or another degu, due to the fact that they are social animals.

Another occasion that can prompt strange behaviour is when the male wants to mate but the female is not receptive. The ritual usually starts with the male sniffing around and sometimes lifting the female's genital area. The female usually objects to this and chuckles at the male. There then follows a period where both animals run round the cage, with the male following the female everywhere. When the female has had enough of this, she will usually make a stand against the male. Both the animals stand bolt upright on their back legs and look like they are boxing. This is always accompanied by lots of noise. The male usually yields to the female and peace returns - until the next time the male's hormones rise! The boxing behaviour may also be seen at foodtime.

Degus can be quite squirrel-like in their behaviour, which is part of their appeal. When eating, they usually sit up on their hind legs, holding their food between their front feet, twisting and turning it as they eat. This may have lead to the degu being given the nickname of 'Chilean Squirrel'.

Degus also enjoy and need a sand bath. Always use chinchilla sand for the dust bath, not any other kind of sand. The sand bath is necessary for the degu to be able to keep his fur clean. If he is denied this, the coat will soon appear oily in texture (a small amount of oil is, however, necessary to waterproof the fur). A sand bath once or twice a week will help to keep your degu's skin and fur healthy and in good condition.

If you allow your degus to run loose, you will have to watch them at all times because they can be quite fearless, which puts them at risk from other pets who may harm them. You will need to degu-proof the area and hazards such as electric cables should be hidden out of sight. Degus are excellent climbers. They can also jump great distances, even from a sitting position, a point to bear in mind when you are holding your degu. They are extremely fast and can literally scale almost any surface. I (JD) have seen my degus run up a wallpapered wall, from the floor to the ceiling.

Catching an escaped degu is not the easiest of tasks and I (JD) have tried many methods over the years. The most successful method to date involves using a 250mm by 200mm aquarium net which I use to trap the degu. I then slide a piece of stiff card under the net, successfully trapping the degu, which allows me to transfer him back to his cage.

## Health

If degus are kept in good clean conditions and their diet is strictly monitored, they do not tend to suffer from many illnesses. However, like any other animal, they are not immune to illness, disease or parasitic invasion. Listed below are all the health problems I (JD) have encountered whilst keeping degus. This list does not claim to be comprehensive. Remember, veterinary treatment should be sought in the case of illness as soon as possible.

### Bites and wounds

From time to time degus may get hurt whilst fighting with each other. Serious wounds should receive veterinary treatment but minor wounds can be dealt with at home. The wounds should be cleaned with a mild disinfectant and both the wound and the animal's enclosure must be kept clean until fully healed. If fighting keeps occurring the degus should be permanently separated.

**Broken limbs**
Degus are extremely agile creatures but, although instances where they break bones are extremely rare, nevertheless it can happen - for instance during an awkward jump. The signs to look for are lack of mobility in a limb, swelling, distress when moving or unnatural movement.

Veterinary attention should be sought immediately; although a cast cannot be put on the affected limb, pain-killing injections can be administered. Although very hard to put into practice, the degu should be kept as quiet as possible until such time as the break heals. One method to help keep your degu quieter is to remove him from his normal enclosure and place him in a single-

Regular handling and observation of your degu should enable you to spot any potential problems.

level cage, where climbing is limited or removed, whilst placing food and water sources close to the animal.

### Broken tooth

Should your degu ever be unfortunate to break one of his front gnawing teeth, there is no need to do anything. As with all other rodents, degu teeth grow constantly throughout the animal's life and a broken tooth will soon re-grow. The only time that it would be necessary to seek the help of your veterinary surgeon would be if the tooth had broken off leaving a sharp jagged edge. Your vet will trim the end off this, leaving the tooth to grow back normally. (see also Overgrown teeth, page 33.)

### Bumblefoot

This is a condition where the paw of the animal swells up and becomes extremely painful. This is usually caused by an animal being kept exclusively on mesh which rubs the skin away from the paw. Infection may then set in rapidly, causing the swelling. A course of antibiotics will be necessary to deal with this problem and the mesh shelving must be covered with timber or some other solid material.

Degus in the wild are unlikely to suffer from Bumblefoot because of their terrain.

### Cataracts

Degus seem very prone to the development of cataracts. A cataract is noticeable as a grey-white covering of the eye. No medical explanation has been given as to why degus seem prone to cataracts but many believe it is caused by inbreeding.

## Colds

Although degus experience extremes of temperature in the wild, they seem very prone to catching colds in captivity. If the cold is not treated and cured as soon as it develops, there is a high risk of pneumonia developing which usually proves fatal to the degu. Breathing becomes difficult for the animal as he cannot blow his nose to clear the mucus. At the first sign of a cold, your degu should be taken to your veterinary surgeon so that a course of antibiotics can be given.

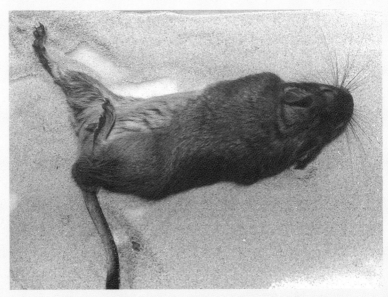

Access to chinchilla sand (for bathing) is vital for your degu's health.

## Diabetes

Degus are highly susceptible to this disease due to their inability to deal naturally with sugars. Unfortunately, it is beyond the scope of the average pet owner to give their pet degu daily insulin injections so, once contracted, this disease usually proves to be fatal. Therefore it really is a case of prevention being better than cure. It is essential that a strict dietary regime is followed and sugary foods such as fruit and raisins are avoided.

The main sign of diabetes is your degu drinking a lot more water than usual. This increase in water intake results in the animal urinating more frequently too.

## Diarrhoea

Degus tend to suffer from diarrhoea when fed too many greens (vegetables). It is easy to tell when a degu has diarrhoea because instead of the normal solid pellet dropping, the animal will pass a watery, smelly substance. If the diarrhoea persists for more than 24 hours, veterinary help should be sought.

The safest foodstuffs to feed are grass, hay, clover and dandelion leaves. Take care to wash thoroughly everything that you pick from your garden or from anywhere else outdoors. Do not pick anything that may have come into contact with insecticides, weed killers and so on. Never pick anything from the roadside as it could be contaminated by car exhaust fumes .

## Liver disease

This illness is of more concern if you have female degus of breeding age. It is usually caused by feeding a diet containing too much fat. The sign of this disease is weight gain by the animal. As far as I know there is no cure for this illness so, once again, it is the duty of the responsible owner to ensure that a healthy diet is provided. Fatty foods such as sunflower seeds and peanuts should only be given as an occasional treat.

## Overgrown teeth

Should the occasion ever arise where the front teeth of your degu grow too long, seek the help of your veterinary surgeon who will trim the teeth with a pair of cutters. Unless you are very experienced, do not try to do this yourself. If you give your degu something to gnaw on, this situation should never arise. I (DGI) have found that a rock or large stone placed in the cage will give the degu something to keep both his teeth and nails worn down.

## Parasites

Degus can get parasites such as mites from other pets (for example, mice or rats). A degu with parasites will scratch and even bite himself. If a degu has tender ears, is losing fur round them or they smell bad, he probably has an ear mite infection.

To treat, obtain mite medication from your vet and follow the instructions.

## Tumours

Degus are no more or no less prone to tumours than any other species of rodent. Most of the cases of tumours that I have come across have been in older animals. There is a general belief that an increased frequency of tumours can be caused through mating related animals.

# BIBLIOGRAPHY

## BIBLIOGRAPHY

At present there are only three degu books on the market - two in German and one in Dutch. These are:

*Unser Degu* by Anna Sporon
Publisher: Kosmos
ISBN 3440061477

*Alles uber Chinchillas und Degus* by Michael Mettler
Publisher: Unknown
ISBN 380681130X

*De cavia en cavia-achtigen als gezelschapsdier* by Anneke Vermeulen-Slik and Rob Dekker
Publisher: Etiko Uitgevers
ISBN 905266126X

## INTERNET

Degu literature can be found on the internet through the following websites:

•Grzimek's Encyclopaedia vol. 3
http://www.blarg.net/~critters/articles/sm_furry/degu.html

•Info about the degu by Heinjan Leliveld
http://home.worldonline.nl/~hleli/deguinfo.html

•Degus by Chris Booton
http://www.geocities.com/Heartland/Prairie/1568/degus.html

•Degus
http://warensburg, k12.mo.us/animals/bretw1/index.html

Degu pictures can be found on the following website:
http://geocities.com/Heartland/Prairie/1568/degupics.html